# KĪLAUE
## and Kauai's National
## Wildlife Refuges

by
David Boynton

A project of Kilauea Point Natural History Association (KPNHA)

Front Cover: Red-footed Booby roosting
in *Casuarina* tree at Kilauea Point, one of
three refuges of the Kaua'i National
Wildlife Refuge Complex.

Previous Page: Red-footed Booby chick
on a nest

This Page: Sunrise at Hanalei National
Wildlife Refuge.

The Donning Company Publishers
184 Business park Drive, Suite 206
Virginia Beach, VA 23462

Steve Mull, General Manager
Barbara B. Buchanan, Office Manager
Richard A. Horwege, Senior Editor
Jeremy Gray, Designer
Stephanie Danko, Imaging Artist
Mary Ellen Wheeler, Proofreader/Editorial Assistant
Scott Rule, Director of Marketing
Travis Gallup, Marketing Coordinator
Anne Cordray, Project Research Coordinator

*Barbara Bolton, Project Director*

**Library of Congress Cataloging in Publication Data**

Boynton, David.
    Kilauea Point and Kauai's national wildlife refuges / by David Boynton.
        p. cm.
    "A project of Kilauea Point Natural History Association."
    ISBN 1-57864-283-3 (soft cover : alk. paper)
    1. Kauai (Hawaii)—Description and travel.  2. Kilauea National Wildlife Refuge
(Kauai, Hawaii)—Description and travel.  3. Kilauea Point (Kauai, Hawaii)—Description
and travel.  I. Kilauea Point Natural History Association (Hawaii)  II. Title.
    DU628.K3B695 2004
    508.969'4—dc22
                                                                2004019435

Printed in the USA at Walsworth Publishing Company

View of Kīlauea Point's historic lighthouse from refuge entrance.

**Rising several hundred feet** above Kīlauea Point (*Wowoni*), the northernmost tip of Kauaʻi, layers of rock clearly reveal the volcanic origins of Crater Hill (*Nihokū*). It was here that Pele, the volcano goddess, came to search for a home where she might live with Lohiʻau, a strong and handsome chief of Hāʻena. Striking her staff into the ground, Pele brought forth a powerful eruption . . . enormous clouds of steam boiled up from the lava as it met cool ocean water, exploding into ash and cinder to form the crater. But these efforts were thwarted by her jealous sister Nāmakaokahaʻi. In anger, the sea goddess generated huge ocean waves that broke away the windward wall of the crater, thus extinguishing Pele's fiery abode. Kauaʻi was not to be her home.

**Three huge stones** are perched near the top of Kīlauea's Crater Hill, a reminder of Pele's anger. Three sisters—Kalama, Pua, and Lāhela—had the audacity to laugh when raging surf was sent forth to douse Pele's fires. Repeating the sisters' names with anger, Pele turned each one to stone with a touch of her staff. Like other legendary stone figures at Hāʻena and on the rim of Kalalau Valley, they stand as a warning of the perils of disrespect. (From F. B. Wichman, *Kauaʻi Ancient Place Names and Their Stories*, 1998)

# Forces of Nature

Softness of water against the hardness of rock: given time, water wins. Given time, even balls of cotton could wear away a boulder, and geology certainly has time on its side. Hawaiian Islands have been forming and eroding for at least 80 million, perhaps even a 100 million years. This is a pittance in geological time, but fully sufficient for ten-thousand-foot-high mountains to erode and subside (at the rate of a tenth of an inch per year) down to sea level reefs, and eventually to form sunken "guyots" such as the Emperor Seamounts at the northern end of the Hawaiian chain.

Powerful surf sweeps into the rocky cove east of Kīlauea Point.

Kīlauea Point is the northernmost point of the main Hawaiian Islands, but extending over three thousand miles farther north to the Aleutians are older Hawaiian Islands, some reduced to atolls or reefs, but most of the them nothing more than highly eroded seamounts lying thousands of feet below the ocean's surface.

All these islands, atolls, and seamounts were created by magma flowing from beneath the ocean floor, originating from a "hotspot"—a plume of magma that has its source hundreds of miles below the earth's surface. As the Pacific tectonic plate moves over the hotspot towards the Aleutian Trench, one island after another is formed. Based on deep-sea core samples from the seamounts, the age of Meiji, closest to the Aleutian Trench, is estimated to be about 80 million years.

Seamounts between Meiji and the above-surface Hawaiian Islands are progressively younger to the south. Midway and Kure, the northernmost of these visible islands, are nearly 30 million years old. Kaua'i and Ni'ihau are about 5 million years old, with the other islands progressively younger: O'ahu with its two volcanoes that are 4 and 3 million years old; Maui, again with two shield volcanoes that are 1.5 and about 1 million years old; and the Big Island (Hawai'i) with its five volcanoes all less than 1 million years old.

Eighteen miles off the eastern coast of the Big Island lies Lo'ihi, thirty-two hundred feet below the ocean surface. In a mere two hundred thousand years, it will rise above the waves to become the next, but not the last, Hawaiian Island.

Kīlauea Stream forms a scenic waterfall at a site not open to public access.

As one of the oldest of the main Hawaiian Islands, Kauai's original form has been highly altered through erosion. Chemical weathering softens the basalt rock that forms the core of the island. The power of water over millions of years became Kauai's sculptor, carving the once-rounded dome of a shield volcano into spectacular valleys and cliffs. Surf nibbles and pounds at the edges. Rainfall eats away at crumbling rock, picks up soil as runoff, gathers force as it collects in streams, and becomes even more powerful as waterfalls that plummet over ledges and cliffs.

Massive faults, slumps, and avalanches have also played a role in creating the Kaua'i we see today, but scientists have differing hypotheses about Kauai's geological history. For example, they are not sure how many shield volcanoes created the island, and until very recently, geologists believed that the steep and spectacular seacliffs of Nā Pali Coast were the result of prodigious landslides where the entire coastline avalanched into the ocean. New evidence supports an older theory that Nā Pali was formed through millions of years of wave-cut erosion.

Scenic viewpoints around the island, such as Kalalau, Hanapēpē, and Hanalei, look into stream-carved valleys on the flanks of Kauai's ancient shield volcano that once rose about 3,000 feet above today's highest point (5,243 feet above sea level).

Kīlauea Stream enters the ocean just east of the refuge boundary.

Kīlauea is one of those valleys, located at the northern edge of the district known as Ko'olau. Kīlauea Stream runs down the center of the valley, and at one point widens above a rocky ledge to form a scenic waterfall that has been featured in several films and commercials. In the classic film *South Pacific*, France Nuyen sang the song "Happy Talk" with John Kerr and Juanita Hall in the chilly waters below a waterfall in Kīlauea Stream.

The stream enters the ocean just east of Crater Hill and Mōkōlea Point at Kāhili Beach, called "Rock Quarry" by local surfers. Kīlauea Point National Wildlife Refuge extends from near Kīlauea Stream, across Mōkōlea Point and the top of Crater Hill, out to the lighthouse at Kīlauea Point.

The Kīlauea Point area has had a complex and exciting volcanic history. At its center, rising 568 feet above sea level, is Crater Hill, which was the vent for lavas that cap the hill and extend west under Kīlauea Point. This eruption occurred about 0.7 million years ago

(Garcia and others, 2004) and like the current eruption of Kīlauea Volcano on the island of Hawai'i, it produced fire fountains giving the rocks at Crater Hill a lumpy appearance.

Crater Hill was built on an older volcano that is similar in size and origin to the famous Diamond Head crater on the island of O'ahu. This older cone was extremely explosive, fragmenting the lava as it erupted into shallow water forming a "tuff cone." This eruption occurred about 1.7 million years ago. Underlying the Crater Hill tuff cone are lava flows that are exposed at Mōkōlea Point (see map). These massive flows, dated at 2.65 million years old, were quarried for building materials. Rock from Mōkōlea Point was used to build the houses on the refuge, and elsewhere in Kīlauea town.

The lower, windward side of the Crater Hill cone is exposed to the tremendous erosional force of huge surf that hits the north shores of all Hawaiian Islands. Kīlauea Point offers one of the greatest (and safest) viewpoints to

Complexity of the volcanic layering is revealed in the northern wall of Crater Hill; a layer of orange-colored clay is sandwiched between the strata.

# Geology of the Kīlauea Point - Crater Hill Area

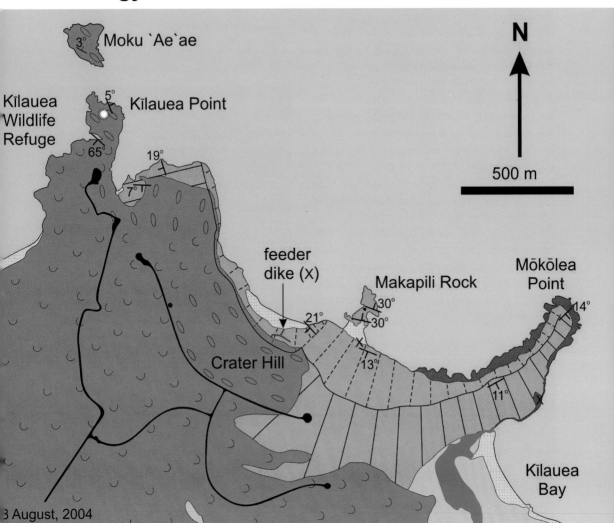

Moku `Ae`ae 3°

Kīlauea Wildlife Refuge

5° Kīlauea Point

65°

19°

7°

N

500 m

feeder dike (X)

Makapili Rock

Mōkōlea Point

30°
30°
21°
13°
14°
11°

Crater Hill

Kīlauea Bay

3 August, 2004

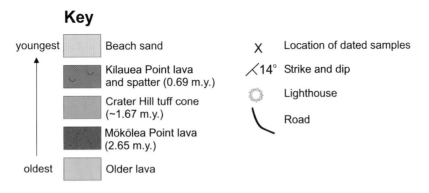

## Key

youngest

oldest

| | |
|---|---|
| Beach sand | |
| Kīlauea Point lava and spatter (0.69 m.y.) | |
| Crater Hill tuff cone (~1.67 m.y.) | |
| Mōkōlea Point lava (2.65 m.y.) | |
| Older lava | |

X — Location of dated samples

⟋14° — Strike and dip

Lighthouse

Road

Geology by M. Garcia, T. Thordarson and D. Wanless, Dept. Geology & Geophysics, Univ. Hawaii at Manoa.

Age dating by T. Tagami and H. Sano, Dept. Geology & Mineralogy, Kyoto University, Japan.

watch this pounding surf, which reaches heights of over thirty feet nearly every winter. Over many hundreds of thousands of years, oceanic forces eroded away the windward side of Crater Hill so that less than half the original structure is still present.

Moku`ae`ae, a small islet that was once connected to Kīlauea Point.

Within the crater lies a collapsed portion of its layered walls, connected to the shoreline by a sandspit or tombolo, and penetrated by a natural arch. On each side of the tombolo lies a small white sandy beach that rarely sees a human footprint.

It's easy to notice the difference in Crater Hill's grayish tuff as compared to the darker black lava from flows that formed Kīlauea Point and the small offshore island Moku'ae'ae, one of more than 100 islets located around the main Hawaiian Islands. At one time, Moku'ae'ae was connected to Kīlauea Point but the connecting portion has eroded away.

The sandy beach which connects a collapsed portion of Crater Hill to the shoreline is called a tombolo.

On the far left of this photo, the darker layers created by volcanic fountaining can be seen overlaying the grayish tuff of Crater Hill.

An interesting feature on Moku'ae'ae is a small blowhole located on the southeastern (closest to the lighthouse) corner. During big winter surf, a geyser of water and spray spouts forth after every large wave. Smaller than the famed landmark known as Spouting Horn in Po'ipū, this blowhole is the product of a lava tube that opens under the ocean's surface.

Compared to lavas of Nā Pali Coast, which date back to 4 or 5 million years ago, the lavas of Kīlauea Point are quite young. They represent the "rejuvenation stage," the final phase of volcanism before a volcano becomes extinct.

Other examples of rejuvenation stage volcanism include the cinder and spatter cones near the Hyatt Regency Resort at Po'ipū. Kauai's last eruptions are thought to have occurred about half a million years ago, although a submarine eruption was reported (but not confirmed) in the channel between the islands of O'ahu and Kaua'i in 1955. However, it appears unlikely that Madam Pele will ever again bring forth her fiery displays on the island of Kaua'i.

# Kīlauea Lighthouse Saved Their Lives

*Night had reached the point where the thin gray edge of day sliced like a knife through the blue-black curtain on the eastern horizon. In a handful of minutes the gleaming points of golden starlight would fade from the sky. Soon the sun would make its usual technicolor entrance on the usual mid-Pacific stage-setting of sky and water. But in the eyes of the two men aboard the plane that had been flying westward throughout the night, one important setting was missing from the stage . . . Land!*

—Hans Christian Adamson, from *Kīlauea Point Lighthouse—The Landfall Beacon on the Orient Run* by Ross R. Aikin, 1988

In May of 1927, a crowd of over one hundred thousand people converged at Le Bourget Airport in Paris to greet the famed aviator Charles Lindbergh, the first person in history to fly solo across the Atlantic Ocean.

Just a month later, a landmark Pacific crossing was under way. As the night of June 28, 1927, turned to dawn, anxiety crept into the cockpit of two U.S. Army fliers who knew they should have already sighted land. The navigational aids of their Focker C-2 aircraft had failed just a few hours after takeoff from San Francisco. Late in the night, two of their three engines had sputtered through a bout of carburetor icing, which was cured by

A tiny point of light from Kīlauea Lighthouse may have been a lifesaver for two pioneering pilots.

dropping from eleven thousand feet to a four-thousand-foot elevation. Celestial navigation helped them through most of the night, but increasing clouds and light rainfall obscured their guiding stars.

Then, what appeared to be a low-lying star near the southeast horizon revealed a conspicuous pattern of double white flashes. From ninety miles away, the pilots turned the *Bird of Paradise* toward Kaua'i, guided by the bright beam from the island's northernmost tip. After circling Kīlauea in the predawn light, Lieutenants Maitland and Hegenberger flew back to Wheeler Field on O'ahu to complete their journey. Were it not for Kīlauea Lighthouse, the first flight across the Pacific from North America to Hawai'i might well have ended in disaster.

A new light, put into working order by volunteers at the lighthouse, has brightened the night sky on commemorative occasions.

# The Northern Light

Ancient Hawaiians were known to use fire as a navigational aid for canoes making their way through reef passages in the darkness of night. One such location is actually a few miles from the shoreline at Kukuiolono (the "light of Lono") in Kalāheo, where bonfires once guided Hawaiian voyagers to land.

As L. Dean states in the book *Lighthouses of Hawai'i* (1991): "All over the world, a fire kindled upon a headland was the first type of navigational aid used by mariners. It soon became obvious that the higher a fire could be placed, the farther out to sea it could be seen."

The earliest known structure built in the islands for navigational purposes was erected in 1840 at Keawaiki on Maui. Nearby, a plaque reads:

*On this site in 1840 King Kamehameha ordered a nine foot wooden tower built as an aid to navigation for the whaling ships anchored off Lahaina.* (Dean, 1991)

A letter written in 1840, translated from its original Hawaiian, describes the Lahaina light as "a tall looking box-like structure, 9 feet high . . . built on a suitable position facing the landing." (Dean, 1991) In 1866, already partially collapsed, the rotting structure was replaced by another wooden lighthouse building.

Just as the Lahaina lighthouses were built for visiting ships, so was the one at Kīlauea Point, but instead of whaling vessels, it would guide merchant ships sailing from Asia to Hawai'i and points farther east. As the northernmost tip of the main Hawaiian Islands, "Ka Lae o Kīlauea" was considered an important landmark for ships sailing on the Orient run.

A bill to authorize survey work for Kīlauea Lighthouse was introduced in 1907 by Prince Jonah Kuhiō Kalaniana'ole, the territorial delegate to Congress. Born in Kōloa on Kauai's south shore, Kuhiō was a highly respected politician and member of the royal family (a great-grandson of Kaumuali'i, Kauai's last king).

Although five years passed before the secretary of the Department of Commerce and Labor issued formal approval of the project,

the actual construction work began just two months later, in July of 1912.

The lighthouse was built on a thirty-one-acre parcel conveyed to the U.S. government by A. B. Spreckels, vice president of Kilauea Sugar Company, in 1909. Originally, this was part of a parcel that consisted of over three thousand acres that Charles Titcomb had purchased from the government of Hawai'i, for the goodly sum of $2,500—less than a dollar an acre. (Today, agricultural land within that three-thousand-acre parcel sells for over $250,000 an acre!)

A grass- and shrub-covered bluff, surrounded on three sides by the ocean, provided an excellent vantage point for the light. Getting the building materials to the site, however, proved quite a challenge. Weather and wave conditions were always a concern, especially since twenty- to thirty-foot-high surf pounds directly on this exposed coastline during winter months.

At first, small boats were rowed from the lighthouse supply ship *Kukui*, anchored in deeper water offshore, into the rocky cove just west of Kīlauea Point, when calm conditions prevailed. The boats tied off to thick cleats cemented into lava rock on shore. The cleats are still there today. Unloading the cargo boats was made easier by rigging a boom ninety feet up on the cliff, to swing loads onto a platform farther uphill.

Construction superintendent Frank Palmer discovered more challenges as work

A boom was rigged to help transport construction materials from the lighthouse tender *Kukui*. (Photograph from National Archives, courtesy of Ross Aikin)

17

commenced. Instead of using the rock directly at the site for concrete work, more suitable gravel had to be purchased from the rock quarry at Mōkōlea Point.

Palmer faced still more difficulties when he learned that the surface on which the lighthouse was to be built was not solid rock as the field survey had indicated, but a porous mix of boulders, gravel, and dirt. Only after digging down eleven feet below ground level was a suitable basalt surface reached. Adapting to the realities of the site, he installed a two-foot-thick concrete slab in an unplanned basement for a solid, load-bearing foundation.

As if building the lighthouse wasn't enough of a challenge, Palmer was also responsible for constructing an "oil storage house, three rubble stone (lava rock) dwellings (keeper residences), three concrete cisterns, a concrete water tank, the steel boom derrick, two miles of water supply line with power pump" and various roadways. (Aikin, 1988) It's a credit to the skill and determination of Palmer that so much of the project, including the lighthouse, was built in just ten months.

The centerpiece of the project was the magnificent "clamshell" Fresnel lens, the "crown jewel" of the lighthouse. Designed and manufactured in France, the lens consisted of several hundred reflecting prisms and refracting glass elements artfully arranged to provide a double flash followed by a delay.

The lens was too heavy—four tons, with its pedestal and rotating mechanism—for ball bearings, so instead it was designed to be "floated" in a vat containing more than 250 pounds of liquid mercury. A "cable and pulley" clockwork mechanism that hung down in a thirty-four-foot-deep shaft rotated the lens, but it required rewinding by hand every three hours, forty minutes. The 250,000-candlepower light, visible from a distance of twenty-one miles out at sea, was provided by an incandescent oil-vapor lamp which sat 217 feet above sea level.

A great community celebration was held at sunset on May 1, 1913, in recognition of the first lighting.

*The Kīlauea Point Lighthouse, like the Cyclops of old, which swept the sea with their one fierce eye, burst forth its shining eye of warning to the mariner . . . while hundreds of country people who had gathered to witness the wonderful sight made the shore and hills ring with astonished delight.* (From the *Garden Island* newspaper in Dean, 1991)

The decades following brought a number of changes to the tedious monotony of ensuring the light performed flawlessly.

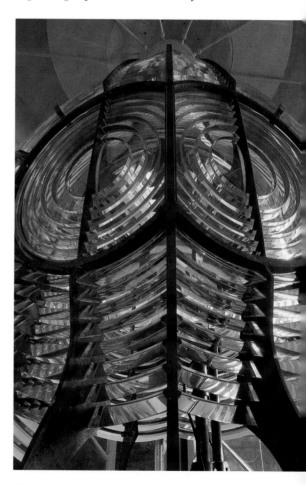

The elegant sculpture of the Fresnel lens greatly intensifies a light beam. This invention provided a very significant improvement in lighthouse capabilities.

In 1929, work commenced on installation of a radio beacon station at Kīlauea Point. When synchronized with the beacon at Makapu'u Point on O'ahu, this station would allow aviators and ships to use two reference points to determine their precise location. The introduction of generators to run the 200-watt radio beacon also provided electricity for the light, resulting in a more than doubling of intensity to 540,000 candlepower. (In 1958, a huge jump in intensity took place, to 2.5 million candlepower, with installation of a 1,000-watt quartz-iodine lamp.)

Kīlauea Point Lighthouse came under administrative control of the Coast Guard in 1939. During World War II, the light and radio beacon of Kīlauea Point were closed down for security reasons. Then, in the 1950s, new technology and the high cost of maintaining lighthouse operations resulted in a national move towards automation.

Despite many lighthouses being automated in the 1950s and 1960s, Kīlauea continued its old ways until 1975, when an attempt at automation failed due to problems

with control and monitoring mechanisms. By February of 1976, a new automated light was put in place atop a ten-foot tower in front of the old lighthouse.

In 1979, the lighthouse and surrounding buildings were placed on the National Register of Historic Places. Although in the mid-1970s the U.S. Fish and Wildlife Service (USFWS) commenced its role of protecting the wildlife at Kīlauea Point, it wasn't until 1985 that the area received its official designation as a National Wildlife Refuge.

To commemorate the Seventy-fifth Anniversary of Kīlauea Point Lighthouse in 1988, the Kīlauea Point Natural History Association commissioned Ross R. Aikin, a meticulous researcher, to produce a book entitled *Kīlauea Point Lighthouse—The Landfall Beacon on the Orient Run*. Its 120 pages are an excellent source of information and images for those interested in learning more.

An automated beacon has taken over for Kīlauea Lighthouse.

# Seabird Sanctuary

They can survive at sea for years at a time, without ever coming to land. But eggs don't float, so come to land they must. For millions of years, uninhabited tropical islands of the Pacific were a safe habitat for nesting seabirds, but as civilization spread across the ocean, islands no longer provided a refuge.

Today, a combination of elements makes Kīlauea Point National Wildlife Refuge the best place on the main Hawaiian Islands to observe seabirds. Six species nest on the refuge, and two others commonly roost here.

A Red-footed Booby chick lacks the bright colors of the adult.

Quality habitat, control of access, and control of predators help to protect the breeding colonies that otherwise might not survive.

Before the arrival of ancient Polynesian voyagers, seabirds almost certainly occurred in great abundance along the coastlines of the main Hawaiian Islands, although at present only remnant populations survive. Introduced predators have taken their toll, human beings and the rats, dogs, and perhaps even the pigs they brought with them. It has been estimated that somewhere between 1 percent and just a tenth of 1 percent of prehuman seabird populations remain on inhabited Hawaiian and other Pacific Islands.

Archaeological research at ancient habitation sites has revealed thousands of seabird bones, indicating that seabirds were an important food source for ancient Hawaiians. Numerous other land bird species—especially flightless ones, some as large as a turkey—were no doubt taken for food, and became extinct before Captain Cook's arrival in 1778.

Estimates of seabird populations from the much smaller (and uninhabited) Northwestern Hawaiian Islands give an indication of what might have occurred there. Laysan, for example, with approximately two miles of shoreline as compared to Kauai's ninety miles, was estimated to have as many as 10 million birds, before a huge decline in their numbers due to the plundering of feather hunters between 1909 and 1915. Tiny Nīhoa was estimated to have a breeding population of half a million seabirds on just one-fourth square mile of land (as compared to Kauai's 552 square miles).

# Seabirds of Kīlauea Point National Wildlife Refuge

Red-footed Booby

Brown Booby

Great Frigatebird

Laysan Albatross

Wedge-tailed Shearwater

Newell's Shearwater

White-tailed Tropicbird

Red-tailed Tropicbird

Some seabird populations have managed to survive by nesting in remote areas. The Hawaiian Petrel, for example, nests in barren lava bluffs up to nearly ten thousand feet on Haleakalā, Maui. On Kaua'i, thousands of Newell's Shearwaters inhabit steep *uluhe* fern-covered slopes of the island's mountainous interior.

On the main Hawaiian Islands, only at Kīlauea Point National Wildlife Refuge do we find a diverse colony of seabirds. The most conspicuous of these is the Red-footed Booby. Although a plain-looking seabird from afar, mostly white with black-edged wings, up close they have an exotic flair with pink facial skin, a pale blue bill, and bright red feet and legs.

True to its name, a booby displays distinctively red feet.

Approaching boobies that are roosting or nesting in the trees and shrubs of Crater Hill will almost always provoke a guttural alarm call: ahhh! Once you hear it, you know why ancient Hawaiians gave this bird the simplest of all Hawaiian names: *'ā*.

Brown Boobies also can be seen along Kauai's coastline. They roost but do not nest on the refuge, and often feed quite close to shore. Their distinctive chocolate brown coloration over back, wings, and head contrasts with the bright white of the breast, like a white shirt under a tuxedo.

Red-footed Boobies joust for position.

Boobies capture their food by plunging into the ocean. Often they feed during the day and return to land in the evening, but before reaching home they must run the gauntlet of hovering frigates.

Great Frigatebirds roost in the curve of Crater Hill (mostly females and juveniles) but are not known to nest on the refuge. As signified by their Hawaiian name, *'iwa*, which translates as "thief," frigates obtain a small portion of their food by stealing it. Like a band of pickpockets looking for a wealthy victim, they wander about offshore from nesting colonies of boobies or other seabirds, stealthily awaiting their return.

Most of the boobies pass through unscathed after a day of fishing, but the *'iwa* seem to know which ones have a meal to share. For these unlucky ones, with a squawk the chase is on, sometimes by just a single *'iwa*, but often by several. The bullying frigates, with strongly hooked bills and a ninety-inch wingspan more than double that of their quarry, harass the boobies, forcing

Six 'iwa are hot on the tail of a Red-footed Booby.

lessly above the surface of waves, their wings bowed and slightly flexed to take maximum advantage of wind currents.

On land, it's a different story. The graceful flyer's gait is clumsy and awkward, earning it the nickname "gooney bird," an epithet that applies equally to the bird's courtship antics. As the birds engage in bouts of head-waving, bobbing, wing-fanning, and preening, they let forth with an amazing assortment of sounds that have been described as a whinny, whine, moo, yammer, snap, and clap.

Laysan Albatross are relatively recent residents of Kīlauea Point National Wildlife Refuge. The first albatross nest was discovered by a local fisherman on the flank of Crater Hill in 1977. Lying on the ground near a chick was the carcass of an adult, apparently killed by a dog. Although hand-fed by refuge personnel, the chick did not survive. Over the years, however, more nests appeared and the population slowly grew.

Efforts were made to attract albatross to the open grassy fields around Kīlauea Point after a predator-proof fence was erected there by members of the Youth and Young Adult Conservation Corps. Painted silhouettes and recorded albatross calls were used, and

them to regurgitate their food. When a fish is dropped into the air, the frigates swoop down to grab it, and a battle of the frigates ensues to see who finally gets the prize.

Frigatebirds are masters of gliding, and are said to have 40 percent more wing surface than any other seabird of similar body weight. They do capture fish from the surface of the water, but since they have difficulty taking off from the ocean's surface, 'iwa don't intentionally land on the water. On the northwestern Hawaiian Islands, they steal nesting material and sometimes pluck downy chicks of other seabirds right from the nest, as well as prey on newly hatched green sea turtles.

The only Kaua'i seabird to have a wing spread close to that of frigatebirds is the Laysan Albatross (*mōlī*). Held aloft by an eighty-inch wingspan, they maneuver effort-

A white chest indicates this is a female frigatebird.

A pair of albatross engage in the courtship antics that helped earn them the name "gooney birds."

Laysan Albatross parents pair for life, and come back to the same nest site each year.

Above: A downy albatross chick.

Left: A Laysan Albatross heads home to Kīlauea Point.

although the birds did not take to their wooden companions, they did begin to nest underneath the ironwood trees west of the Point. The population of Laysan Albatross within the refuge is now over two hundred birds, many of which can be seen during spring and summer on "Albatross Hill" with the viewing scopes near the lighthouse.

Albatross lay just one egg per year in a nest that is often little more than a scraped-out bowl on bare dirt. Since they are ground-nesting birds and have no innate fear of predators, those that nest outside of the protective fence are vulnerable to predation by dogs and cats. This also holds true for Wedge-tailed Shearwaters or 'ua'u kani, which nest in burrows one- to three-feet deep that they dig with clawed feet into the dirt. They also take advantage of rock crevices and natural overhangs, such as small ledges or roots.

There are a few colonies that survive on the main islands other than Kaua'i, including a colony along the road of an affluent community at Black Point, on the slopes of Diamond Head. In areas like this, where they nest in rocky crevices, they may be out of the reach of probing dogs. However, mongooses are a major predator, and Kauai's comparative abundance of shearwater colonies is partly the result of the island being, so far, mongoose-free. Where they are not protected by rocky crevices or the refuge's fence, most colonies have been decimated by dogs.

People are also a problem for nesting shearwaters. Unknowing or unconcerned trekkers often step on and collapse the burrows, thus literally burying the birds alive.

Many a story has emerged from the nighttime calls of Wedge-tailed Shearwaters, which are also known as the "moaning birds." Among the ghostly sounds that emanate from their colonies, often hidden among coastal shrubbery, are sounds that have been compared to a baby crying. This can create a weird sensation for an unsuspecting person on a moonlight stroll along the beach.

Another shearwater species, the Newell's Shearwater, or 'a'o, is found at Kīlauea Point, but there are only a couple of nests. Eggs of this threatened species were transplanted from their traditional breeding grounds in Kauai's mountainous interior, and put under nesting Wedge-tailed Shearwaters, a process known as cross-fostering.

In places where they are not protected by rocks or fences, Wedge-tailed Shearwaters are very vulnerable to predation by dogs. More than fifty dead shearwaters were found at this colony, a couple of miles east of Kīlauea.

Wedge-tailed Shearwater chick outside its burrow.

Some of the transplanted birds survived, and appear to have created a second generation that adds its unusual sounds—akin to the braying of a donkey—to the moans of wedge-tails. Fledgling Newell's Shearwaters are easily confused by power lines and bright lights; as a result, hundreds of these birds crash into buildings and onto roadways around Kaua'i. A very successful recovery program, S.O.S. or "Save Our Shearwaters," has been instituted. People who find downed shearwaters can place them in protective boxes located at fire stations around the island. The recovered birds are later released from a safe location. Still, their population has dropped off precipitously during the past two decades.

Shearwaters, petrels, and other ground-nesting birds are very vulnerable to predation, but the White-tailed Tropicbird, or *koa'e kea*, has a survival strategy to avoid this problem. They nest in areas that are highly inaccessible, vertical cliff faces where no predators can tread, except perhaps for the occasional rat.

Sometimes called the "canyon birds" because they are often seen flying over inland valleys including Waimea Canyon, tropicbirds are angelic and graceful in flight, seeming to float on the winds just for the pleasure of it.

They are mostly white with a black bar across the top of the wings, and two long, white central tail feathers. A relative, the Red-tailed Tropicbird, or *koa'e' ula*, is similar in appearance but has red central tail feathers, no black streak on the back, and a bright red bill (instead of yellow).

The area round Kīlauea Point National Wildlife Refuge is the only place on Kaua'i where the red-tails nest. Unlike the inland-nesting white-tails, they stay close to the shoreline, laying a single egg under boulders, natural overhangs, or hidden in vegetation. The adult birds are very conspicuous during the middle of the day when they congregate in small groups, exchanging raucous calls with their mates as they fly upwards and backwards, circling around one another just offshore from the lighthouse. They also tuck their wings and soar down the cliffs to check on their mates or a chick in the nest.

The long central tail feathers of the two tropicbird species were used by ancient Hawaiians for *kāhili*, a wooden staff with feathers mounted along the top portion, which accompanied processions of royalty.

Seabirds continue to play an important role for today's Hawaiians. They are the "eyes of the fisherman." From their vantage point high above the ocean's surface they can look down and see the schools of fish beneath. Small fish are food for large fish such as *'ahi, mahimahi,* and *ono,* but when chased to the surface, they also become food for seabirds.

By following seabird "piles" and observing their behavior, skilled fishermen can tell what's going on beneath the ocean's surface miles away. For this reason, the survival of our island seabirds is especially important to many local people; without these eyes in the sky, their ability to bring home fish for the family or for commercial sale would be greatly reduced.

A White-tailed Tropicbird soars down the cliff face of Crater Hill, while a red-tail does a close fly-by at Kīlauea Point.

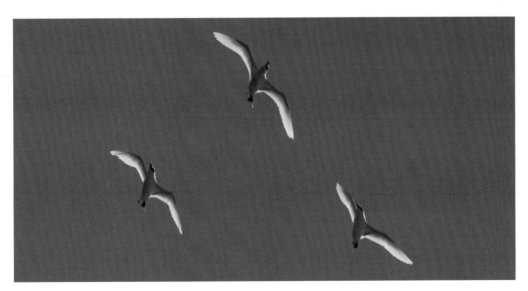

Red-tailed Tropicbirds offer quite a show during the summer at Kīlauea Point, sometimes flying upwards and backwards as they interact in small groups.

# Nēnē: Hawaii's State Bird

Kīlauea Point National Wildlife Refuge has become one of the primary nesting sites for Hawaii's State Bird, the *nēnē* or Hawaiian Goose, an endemic species that occurs naturally only in Hawai'i. Related to the Canada Goose, they are smaller, and have a distinctive pattern of diagonal rows of dark furrows in the neck feathers.

*Nēnē* are a recent introduction to the refuge. In the 1950s, it was estimated that there were only about thirty *nēnē* left in the wild. Efforts began to breed the *nēnē* in captivity and release the young into the wild on the Big Island, and later at remote areas of Haleakalā National Park on Maui, which provided grassland and shrubland habitat on lava fields, similar to that on the Big Island.

Though there is no written record of *nēnē* on Kaua'i in historical times, fossil evidence from south shore coastal dunes indicates they once lived here. In 1991, a dozen birds were introduced to a protected area at the top of Crater Hill, and as biologists realized that *nēnē* prospered in this habitat, twenty more birds were introduced over the next couple of years.

Today, Kauai's *nēnē* population is thriving—an estimated 650 birds. They can be seen on golf courses, taro field dikes, pastures, and grassy fields like those on Crater Hill. Perhaps their preferred habitat is coastal lowlands, rather than high-elevation lava fields. People should not feed *nēnē*, for these endangered birds need to have a healthy caution for humans and associated dangers (such as dogs and cars).

Furrowed neck feathers are a distinguishing feature of the Hawaiian Goose.

# Native Plant Life

Unusual as it may seem, Hawaii's coastline and beaches—even where humans have left big urban footprints—are often good places to find native plants. It's a matter of adaptation, the ability of living organisms to survive in their natural habitat.

Shoreline habitats are a tough place for plants—wind exposure, salt spray, low-nutrient sand or bare rock, burning sun, and the occasional bout of a saltwater soaking when the surf comes up. But coastal plants have lived in these conditions for millions of years, and are specially adapted to survive there. Take a coastal plant up to the rainforest and it will probably die, just as a rainforest plant will not survive life on the beach.

The Hawaiian Islands are home to more than a thousand native species of flowering

Adapted to wind and salt spray, native coastal vegetation predominates on the offshore islet Mokuʻaeʻae.

plants. These natives, which were here before the arrival of humans, can be divided into two groups: indigenous and endemic. About 90 percent are endemic to the islands; they evolved here and occur naturally only here. The remaining 10 percent are indigenous, meaning that they are native to Hawaiʻi but also occur naturally in other areas.

Plants from coastal areas are more likely than inland species to be indigenous, for they can survive in salt water and hence travel more easily from island to island. One such plant, probably the most abundant native species at Kīlauea Point, is *naupaka kahakai*, which is widespread throughout the tropical Pacific. It has a white fleshy "fruit" (mesocarp) that *nēnē* like to eat. Within is a hard but lightweight seed coat which protects the seed and allows it to float without harm on ocean currents.

Eight other *naupaka* species have evolved in the islands. One of these is a single-island endemic that grows on Big Island lava flows. Another is an endangered "dwarf" *naupaka* that inhabits coastal dunes on Maui and small islets off Molokaʻi. The others—called *naupaka kuahiwi* or "mountain *naupaka*"—are endemic to two or more main Hawaiian Islands. A Kauaʻi legend tells of a young man and his sweetheart who incurred the wrath of their *kumu hula* (their hula teacher, Kilioe). The young couple tried to escape, but Kilioe caught and killed the young woman at Lumahaʻi; the young man suffered the same fate on a mountain ridge above. Laka, goddess of hula, turned them into living plants—a beach *naupaka* and a mountain *naupaka*—each with just half a flower, forever separated.

# Native Plants of Kīlauea Point National Wildlife Refuge

Naupaka kahakai

ʻIlima kū kahakai

ʻŪlei

Nēhē

ʻĀheahea

ʻAkoko

Hala

Ālula

Although the plants look quite different, the flowers of beach *naupaka* (left) and mountain *naupaka* (right) have a distinctive similarity in form.

*Naupaka* shrubs form dense hedges around Kīlauea Point that provide excellent cover for Wedge-tailed Shearwaters nesting beneath the tangled branches. The plant is also useful to local residents who pick a couple of leaves before going snorkeling. A waxy covering on the leaves helps retain moisture and protects the inner leaf tissues from salt damage. Wiping the leaves with a little water around the inside of a facemask helps prevent the glass from fogging up.

Another coastal plant still used by local people is *'ilima kū kahakai*. A diminutive member of the hibiscus family, the pale orange flowers—thin as paper—are strung together to make the island *lei* of O'ahu. Hundreds of flowers must be picked early in the morning for just one *lei*, a special gift indeed. June is a good time to see *lei'ilima*, as they are worn by horses and *pa'u* riders representing the island of O'ahu each year in the Kamehameha Day Parade.

When growing near the shore, *'ilima* hugs the ground, forming a mat that lessens the exposure to windblown salt spray. Inland, away from dessicating winds, it grows as a small shrub or bush. Native plants, such as *'ilima kū kahakai*, are used at some residential and resort properties as groundcovers, especially near the coastline, for they are hardy natural survivors that need little care.

*'Ūlei*, an indigenous member of the rose family, forms a thick tangle near the coastline, but grows to ten feet tall on inland sites. It can be recognized by dark green compound leaves and small, white flowers. Seeds and young leaves were used medicinally by ancient Hawaiians, the hard wood made into spears, and supple branches woven into conical fish traps.

Not all coastal plants are small shrubs or groundcovers. The *hala* or *Pandanus* tree, which grows over thirty feet tall, is found throughout the northern Pacific to northern Australia. There are separate male and female trees, the latter with large compound fruits that look superficially like a pineapple. Each of these consists of forty to eighty drupes, which can drift on the sea from island to island. The drupes are used to make *lei*, and are eaten in some parts of the Pacific.

Hundreds of *'ilima* flowers go into each *lei*, here worn by a *pa'u* rider representing the island of O'ahu during the annual Kamehameha Day Parade.

*Hala* leaves (*lauhala*), after the spines were stripped from leaf edges, provided ancient Hawaiians with an excellent material for weaving into mats and sails. The leaves were also used for thatch for dwellings. *Lauhala* mats are still popular in local homes, and a wide variety of other products can also be found in shops and craft fairs—bracelets, purses, hats, and varied containers.

Proof of *hala*'s native status was discovered on the rocky coastline at Waikoko, on the west side of Hanalei Bay. An imprint of a *hala* fruit was discovered in a huge lava boulder hundreds of thousands of years old. Thus, *hala* predates humans who have been here on the islands for less than two thousand years.

Several endemic plant species found at Kīlauea Point are special—they live naturally nowhere else. The Hawaiian Islands, with mid-ocean isolation and a tremendous variety of habitats—from tropical shorelines dry as a desert through deep-soiled valleys to rainforests and bogs, barren lava flows, and snow-covered mountains—proved a perfect laboratory for evolution to occur. The result: 90 percent of Hawaii's native flowering plant species are endemic, as are 99 percent of native insects, land snails, and land birds. This rate of endemism is the highest in the world, making Hawai'i an internationally renowned center for the study of evolution.

There are over twenty "cousins" of *nēhē* (in the endemic genus *Lipochaeta*) that are endemic to Hawai'i. The *nēhē* at Kīlauea Point has succulent leaves to help preserve moisture, and small yellow flowers. Where exposed to the wind on the top of Crater Hill, it grows as a ground-spreading mat but becomes a shrub in more protected areas.

*'Akoko*, in the *Euphorbiaceae* family, has over a dozen endemic relatives. *Koko* means "blood" in Hawaiian, and may refer to the white milky sap that oozes out of *'akoko* (and other *Euphorbs*) when cut or broken off.

Just one species of *Chenopodium* (a genus known as "lamb's quarters") evolved in the islands. Known as *'āheahea*, this endemic shrub is used for nesting material by Red-footed Boobies.

Most of the *hala* trees at Kīlauea Point were planted, but they grow naturally in abundance along Nā Pali Coast.

Two endemics, *nēhē* and *'akoko*, are among the many native species planted on the refuge by USFWS staff, interns, and volunteers.

# Ālula: Endangered Cliff Dweller

To scientists around the world, Hawai'i provides the finest examples for a type of evolution known as "adaptive radiation," where many different species evolve from one. Here, it's like Darwin's famed finches times ten.

Botanist Ken Wood searches for *alula* in their natural habitat on Nā Pali Coast cliffs. Less than a dozen individuals remain from the original populations.

People readily recognize *Lobelias* as pretty little flowers growing in their home garden, but in the natural gardens of Hawaii's forests and shrublands over one hundred endemic species of *Lobelioids* evolved from one ancestor that arrived millions of years ago.

Many of these have curved flowers that are a perfect fit for curved bills of endemic forest birds. They are interdependent, a perfectly obvious and visible example of the millions of interdependencies that exist hidden in our natural island ecosystems.

*Ālula* is a unique Hawaiian *Lobelioid* that appears to be adapted for moth rather than bird pollination. It evolved from a different ancestor than the one that produced more than one hundred species. There are two endemic species of *ālula* (*Brighamia*), one on Molokai's windward seacliffs, and the other known from Kauai's Nā Pali Coast, Hā'upu mountains, and coastal cliffs of Ni'ihau.

Shaped somewhat like a baseball bat with a head of cabbage on top, these plants have become extremely rare in their cliffside habitat. It is thought that, in addition to competition from invasive weeds and munching goats, the gradual disappearance of a native moth that once pollinated the plant is a major link to their highly endangered status.

Botanists have rappelled down steep cliffs to fill in for the missing pollinator, and by hand-pollinating the flowers, have helped produce the seeds from which the *ālula* plants at Kīlauea Point have grown. They have been planted near the walkway just before the interpretive center, into an artificially made habitat that is quite similar to their natural Nā Pali home.

A planted garden of *ālula* plants near the Visitor Center.

33

# Ocean Wildlife

If the soaring seabirds and scenic vistas of Kīlauea Point don't make your day, there's always the opportunity for an interesting visual encounter with ocean wildlife. From 180 feet above the waves, visitors have an excellent vantage point over quite an expanse of ocean.

Winter and early spring are the only times of the year when you have a chance for the grand slam: seeing a humpback whale, spinner dolphin, green sea turtle, and Hawaiian monk seal. It's a rare experience for this to occur at Kīlauea Point, but a possibility.

Although three of the species stay in nearshore waters throughout the year, humpback whales are migratory, arriving in Hawaiian waters around November and departing in late spring. Their summer months are spent in Alaskan waters, where extremely productive ocean upwellings provide the hundreds of pounds of food—sometimes as much as a ton—that they consume each day.

Humpbacks, or *koholā*, are more frequently seen in Kaua'i waters during the spring months, before they migrate back to Alaska. It appears that some of the whales that winter around the more southerly Hawaiian Islands pass northwards up the island chain before departing to Alaska, hence they're seen here later in the season.

Occasionally, humpbacks will come within a few hundred yards of the shoreline at Kīlauea Point, but more often they're a mile or more offshore. Still, they're a pleasure to observe, and a challenge to one's patience, since they sometimes spend many minutes underwater before surfacing. Varied behaviors such as spy hopping, tail slapping, pectoral displays, and breaching can be seen when the whales are active. At other times, it's just dorsal fins and blows as they cruise past the point, but even then it's still fun to predict where their next surfacing will occur.

The waters off Kīlauea Point are part of the Hawaiian Islands Humpback Whale National Marine Sanctuary, a designation that primarily focuses on protecting this endangered species through educational programs.

The Hawaiian monk seal, another endangered marine mammal, not only swims close to shore but will sometimes haul out on the rocky shoreline, usually in the cove east of the lighthouse. They come ashore to snooze, unlike dolphins and whales that sleep in the ocean. They are often seen alone, solitary as a monk, hence the name "monk" seal.

*Koholā*, the humpback whale. (Photo by Tim DeLaVega, www.napaliphoto.com)

Endangered Hawaiian monk seals come ashore to sleep.

They are among the rarest seals in the world, with less than fifteen hundred surviving. The Mediterranean monk seal is even more rare, with less than a thousand in existence, and the Caribbean monk seal is extinct, with the last individual sighted in 1952.

Most Hawaiian monk seals live and breed in the waters of the Northwestern Hawaiian Islands National Wildlife Refuge, a lengthy stretch of small islands, reefs, and atolls extending over a thousand miles to Midway and Kure. The refuge was created in 1909 by President Theodore Roosevelt to protect their vast colonies of seabirds and other marine life.

Protective legislation requires that people stay a sufficient distance away so as not to disturb sleeping monk seals, which come ashore on rocky shores and sandy beaches all around Kaua'i, even at the island's most populous beach parks. They are especially sensitive after they have given birth. If excessively disturbed, the nursing mother may leave the pup, which might well lead to its death. Over the past decade, there has been an average of one or two pups born each year on Kaua'i.

Known as '*īlio-holo-i-ka-uaua* in Hawaiian, a name that translates as "dog that runs in the rough (seas)," they eat up to one-fifth their body weight in food each day, including eels, fish, octopus, and lobsters. Females, which grow larger than males, may reach eight feet in length and weigh up to six hundred pounds. They are amazing divers, with the ability to go down to depths of over a thousand feet and stay underwater for twenty minutes.

A third marine mammal sometimes spotted in the waters off Kīlauea Point is the spinner dolphin or *nai'a*. Although not on the

A mother monk seal and pup on a north shore beach.

A pod of spinner dolphins is often seen off the Kīlauea shoreline.

endangered species list, they are protected by the Marine Mammal Protection Act. Under this act, it is unlawful to harass any marine mammal. Harassment includes doing something that causes a marine mammal to change its behavior. Although it has become popular to swim with the dolphins, people should avoid disturbing the natural rhythm and activity of dolphins, seals, and whales.

Spinners are found throughout the oceans of the world, from tropical to temperate waters. They reach a length of six and a half feet, and may weigh up to two hundred pounds. Their upper and lower jaws are lined with about two hundred sharply pointed teeth.

These great "bow-riders" often approach very close to fishing or tour boats, looking playfully fearless just inches in front of the hull. True to their name, they spontaneously jump into the air in what appears to be playful bliss, and can complete numerous spins during a single jump.

A pod of spinner dolphins is frequently seen cruising leisurely within a few hundred yards of the shoreline between 'Anini Beach and Kīlauea. Apparently, most of their feeding occurs at night.

Green sea turtles or *honu*, on the other hand, regularly feed during the day, and can be seen close to shore at many locations around Kaua'i nibbling on algae that grows on rocky coastlines or reefs. The "green" in the turtle's name comes, not from the shell color (which is mottled brown) but from the green color of its body fat.

A spinner lives up to its name.

Green sea turtles are found throughout the world's oceans. The Hawaiian population appears to be genetically distinct from other Pacific green sea turtles. They have been listed as a threatened species by the federal government, and are also protected by state law.

Ninety percent of Hawaii's green sea turtles come ashore to nest on the sandy islets of French Frigate Shoals, located about eight hundred miles northwest of Kaua'i. During the egg-laying season, which peaks in June to July, females dig a hole above the high waterline and lay from 100 to 120 eggs. Hatchlings will emerge about sixty days later, but it is a mystery where they go until they appear as juveniles several years later around the main Hawaiian Islands.

Adult turtles reach four feet in length and may weigh up to four hundred pounds. They first breed when about twenty-five years old and can live up to eighty years.

Nearly half the green sea turtles around the main Hawaiian Islands have a disease called fibropapillomatosis, which causes tumors to grow—sometimes as large as a grapefruit—over a turtle's eyes, or on the mouth, neck, or flippers. The disease is most prevalent where humans have impacted coastal waters.

Years ago, turtles were seen daily resting

Fibropapilloma tumors on a Nā Pali green sea turtle.

in the cove east of the lighthouse, but in recent years they have been less consistent visitors. Fortunately, they do nest on remote beaches of Kaua'i and the population is gradually recovering.

*Honu* sometimes show little fear of humans, but they are a protected species and should not be disturbed.

# Wetlands and Waterbirds

In the traditions of ancient Hawai'i, the first taro plant was the elder "brother" of Hāloa, progenitor of the Hawaiian people. Taro is also identified with Kāne, the "primordial god of procreative life." (from *Native Planters in Old Hawai'i* by Handy and Handy, 1972) Thus, there is a special reverence for taro by Hawaiians, ancient and modern, for its sacred status and also because it was the staple food of the islands.

Tremendous effort went into the production of taro, which shaped the "political geography" of the islands. Valley floors were laid out in a checkerboard network of wetland taro patches, generally lined by stone walls and interspersed with ditches (*auwai*). An exemplary cooperative effort to farm the taro by families who lived within a watershed

Koloa ducklings at Hanalei National Wildlife Refuge.

(*ahupua'a*) became a central core of Hawaiian culture throughout the islands, wherever sufficient water was available.

In the decades following Captain Cook's arrival on the islands, tremendous changes took place to this "man-made" ecosystem. In the mid-1800s, prime agricultural lands were converted to the production of sugar cane. When water was diverted to irrigate these fields, taro patches were left dry. Also, rice production displaced taro farming throughout much of Hawai'i. In the late 1800s and early 1900s, huge areas of wetland habitat were drained and filled for urban development.

With all this change, populations of five native waterbird species, which are dependent on both the natural and man-made wetland habitats, have suffered serious declines. Four of the five species are listed as endangered by the state and federal government: the Hawaiian Stilt (*ae'o*), Hawaiian Coot ('*alae ke'oke'o*), Hawaiian Moorhen ('*alae 'ula*), and Hawaiian Duck (*koloa maoli*). For their protection, a number of state and federal wildlife refuges have been created throughout the islands.

Hanalei National Wildlife Refuge is the prime wetland refuge in Hawai'i. Known for its scenic beauty as well as prolific taro production, the 917-acre Hanalei National Wildlife Refuge includes about 186 acres used for taro production, and 62 acres of managed ponds and wetlands.

Through a cooperative farming agreement with the U.S. Fish and Wildlife Service

(USFWS), taro farmers on the refuge are allowed to continue farming because their wet fields provide feeding habitat for endangered waterbirds. It's a win-win situation, the endangered birds being the ultimate beneficiary. The farmers have benefited by enjoying very reasonable lease rates for their land, by extensive improvements to the ditch system, and by a large increase in land made available for taro farming since the refuge was established in 1972.

An aerial photo of Hulē'ia National Wildlife Refuge.

In turn, the farmers must employ farming practices which are compatible with waterbird protection. They must care for waterbirds by controlling household pets such as cats and dogs and by not harming waterbird nests. During harvest, for example, they leave in place some of the taro surrounding any nests found in their *lo'i kalo* (taro patches).

A second wetland refuge, Hulē'ia National Wildlife Refuge, is located in the Līhu'e area about a mile inland from Nawiliwili Harbor, just above the Menehune Fishpond (*'Alekoko*). There is no taro farming at Hulē'ia; instead,

View of Hanalei National Wildlife Refuge from Hanalei Overlook near Princeville Shopping Center.

A view from the taro fields at Hanalei National Wildlife Refuge.

mowing and discing of the marshy grassland near the river creates excellent habitat and cover for waterbirds.

Ducks Unlimited, an international wetlands conservation organization based in

Wetlands management creates quality habitat for endangered waterbirds, like these *koloa maoli*.

Memphis, Tennessee, has partnered with the U.S. Fish and Wildlife Service in habitat enhancement projects on Kaua'i. Also, field research is being conducted that seeks to discover what water levels, food plants, aquatic invertebrates, and other variables provide optimum habitat.

To minimize disturbance to endangered waterbirds, access for visitors is restricted on the two refuges. However, the native waterbirds can be viewed at several points along the roadways in Hanalei, where taro patches are close to the road.

Two of Hawaii's four endangered waterbirds (moorhen and stilt) are actually subspecies that are closely related to their North American counterparts. The Hawaiian Coot was considered a subspecies until 1993, when the American Ornithological Union classified it as a separate species from the very similar American Coot. The *koloa maoli* or Hawaiian Duck, also classified as a full species, is quite similar to the mallard, its progenitor. A fifth native waterbird, the Black-crowned Night Heron or *'auku'u*, is presumably the most recently arrived of the species, and has not differentiated from its mainland counterparts.

Rarest of these waterbirds is the Hawaiian Moorhen (*'alae 'ula*). In the 1940s, a statewide population count revealed less than 60 individuals. Their numbers have recovered over the decades, but the species is still very rare, with recent counts ranging from 250 to 300 birds.

The moorhen (a.k.a. Hawaiian Gallinule) is dark gray with a black head and neck, white

*Koloa maoli* are sometimes seen resting along taro patch dikes. (Photo by Vernon Byrd, USFWS)

feathers on the side and under the tail, and a blood-red frontal shield. According to Hawaiian lore, to reveal the secret of fire held by 'alae 'ula, the demigod Maui rubbed its forehead so hard that it bled.

'Alae 'ula have yellowish-green feet with long toes that are adapted to walking on soft mud and even floating aquatic vegetation, such as nonnative water lilies. At Hanalei, the birds are often seen wading through the shallow water among the taro plants. They are adept swimmers, and can be seen in Hanalei River and other streams on Kaua'i.

Some of Hawaii's moorhens have adapted to human presence and can be seen at resorts, golf courses, agricultural fields, and other areas where there are suitable aquatic habitats. However, their daring is a survival problem. Where people are present, so are vehicles, dogs, and other hazards, and human presence near a nest will sometimes cause an incubating bird to abandon.

'Alae ke'oke'o, the Hawaiian Coot, is dark gray like the moorhen but easily distinguished by its white bill and frontal shield, green legs and feet, and lack of white undertail feathers. Their toes, fitted with scalloped webbing, look almost reptilian. Hawaiian Coots are primarily swimmers, and prefer the open water of fresh and brackish ponds, and wetland impoundments.

Hawaiian Moorhen are more likely to be seen wading in shallow water.

People are amazed to discover that Hawaii's coot is an endangered species, since its mainland "cousin" is so abundant. The statewide population has been estimated at

Photo by Brenda Zaun, USFWS

Hawaiian Coots are swimmers that prefer open water habitats.

between two thousand and four thousand birds. Difficulty in pinning this estimate down may be the result of the coot's migratory patterns. The Kaua'i birds, for example, fly over to the island of Ni'ihau during wet years to utilize the hundreds of acres of intermittent lakes there.

Kaua'i is home to about 80 percent of the state's population of koloa maoli, the Hawaiian Duck, which has a statewide population of about twenty-five hundred birds. Restoration efforts helped reestablish and maintain populations on O'ahu and the Big Island.

Koloa maoli inhabit low elevation wetlands, taro fields, and river valleys. They are also found in mountain streams, creating quite a surprise when flushed by an unsuspecting hiker. Both male and female are mottled brown in color, with orange legs and feet. When in flight, the trailing edge of the wing is striped with bright blue or green, bordered by white.

The decline in numbers of koloa was caused by a combination of many impacts such as loss of habitat, invasive plants in their habitat, predation, and also, into the 1900s, hunting.

*Ae'o, the Hawaiian Stilt, in a taro field.*

More recently, hybridization with mallards has become a problem, especially for the populations outside of Kaua'i.

*Koloa maoli* are often seen at Hanalei National Wildlife Refuge in the wetlands, and on the dikes between taro patches. They are very wary birds, and unlike the *nēnē*, which is quite fearless in the presence of people, they are readily disturbed by approaching humans. This attribute ultimately benefits their chance of survival.

*Ae'o*, the Hawaiian Stilt, is easily recognized by its long, pink legs. Similar to the Black-necked Stilt of North America, the Hawaiian subspecies has more black on the head and neck, and a slightly longer bill. They stand about sixteen inches tall.

Stilts are waders, usually found in marshy areas, feeding in flooded or shallow taro patches and on mudflats. With their narrow tweezer-like bills, they pick worms, snails, insects, and other tiny aquatic invertebrates from the mud.

At Hanalei, they primarily nest on the undisturbed mudflats of the refuge's ponds and impoundments. During their breeding season, *ae'o* will often be heard before being seen. They offer a distinctive "keek" sound when disturbed, and will defend their nesting area by dive-bombing the predator, including humans. Sometimes, to draw a human or a predator away, an adult bird will hobble away

Hawaiian Stilt eat tiny invertebrates that live in mudflats and shallow water habitats.

from its nest or young, holding its wing as if it were broken.

An estimate in the 1990s put the statewide population at twelve hundred to sixteen hundred birds, with Kaua'i, O'ahu, and Maui supporting over 90 percent. Like the coots, Kauai's stilts sometimes migrate seasonally to Ni'ihau to take advantage of the extensive shallow water habitat during rainy years.

*'Auku'u* patiently stalk or stand still to await their prey.

The Black-crowned Night Heron (*'auku'u*) is much larger than the four other native waterbirds. The species is distributed throughout North America, South America, Africa, and Eurasia. They are gray and white birds, black on the back and bill, with two or three long white head plumes. Standing over two feet tall, with nearly a four-foot wingspan, the *'auku'u* is a silent stalker. They wait motionlessly, deep orange-colored eyes on the lookout for small fish, frogs, or aquatic invertebrates, which they grab with a quick strike from a sharp beak. They also are known to

eat mice and the downy young of Hawaii's endangered waterbirds.

*'Auku'u* have caused problems for aquaculturists at sites where shrimp and prawns are raised. Populations of this indigenous waterbird reach unnaturally high levels with the abundant food source in open ponds. *'Auku'u* can be seen at many locations on Kaua'i, including reef flats, marshes, ditches, taro fields, and streams. Their distinctive croaking sound—"quark"—is occasionally heard during the day or night.

Many other species visit Hawaii's wetlands, including migratory waterfowl and shorebirds. More than two dozen species of ducks and geese have been recorded in the islands, with pintails and shovelers being the most abundant winter migrants.

The Pacific Golden-Plover, *kōlea*, is the most frequently seen shorebird on Kauai's wildlife refuges. Other shorebirds such as wandering tattlers and ruddy turnstones inhabit shorelines, exposed reef flats, and shallow wetland habitats. These species are winter residents that migrate north for the spring and summer breeding season.

Pacific Golden-Plover are the most abundant of the islands' migratory shorebirds.

# Into the Future

Hawai'i has the dubious distinction of being the nation's (if not the world's) endangered species capital. The statistics supporting this are shocking.

Of 115 known species of endemic Hawaiian landbirds, only 8 are not endangered or extinct. More than half are

The Hawaiian Goose, a Kīlauea Point National Wildlife Refuge success story.

known only from fossil evidence—species that probably became extinct during Polynesian habitation of the islands before Captain Cook's arrival. Forty-five others have become endangered or extinct during the past two centuries.

Native Hawaiian plants have also suffered disturbing losses. With just one-tenth of 1 percent of the nation's land area, Hawai'i is home to 40 percent of its threatened and endangered plants.

The challenge to perpetuate these species seems overwhelming, but without concerted, continuing effort the extinctions will continue. Each species lost is another tiny hole in the hull of our proverbial spacecraft, planet earth. How many losses can we take before (eco)systems start to break down?

The threats to survival of unique Hawaiian ecosystems are similar to those in other places. However, because of the tremendous diversity packed into a tiny area and the forgiving isolation in which Hawaiian species evolved, the islands are more sensitive to change than continental areas.

There are success stories, and amongst these the recovery of Hawaii's *nēnē* is a prominent one. From a population that had dwindled to near extinction, with only around thirty *nēnē* surviving in the wild, they now number over a thousand, and have formed wild breeding populations at many different locales.

Kīlauea Point itself has shown a remarkable ecological improvement since the U.S. Fish and Wildlife Service initiated work projects there in the mid-1970s. Much of its native vegetation including *hala* trees, *naupaka*, and other coastal shrubs was planted by Youth and Young Adult Conservation Corps workers, and refuge volunteers, in what used to be a landscape full of invasive alien plants. Seabird populations have also dramatically increased with protection and management of the refuge.

The National Wildlife Refuge System is continuing to expand its presence across America to protect the nation's biological heritage. It has a strong presence in the Hawaiian Islands, with a total of ten refuges that range from coastal marshes to mid-elevation rainforests. Largest of these is the huge Northwestern Hawaiian Islands National Wildlife Refuge, which consists of a chain of islands, reefs, and atolls extending over a thousand miles in a northwesterly direction from the main Hawaiian Islands.

Including Hawai'i, there are currently 545 refuges in the National Wildlife Refuge System. These offer a lifetime of opportunities to explore and learn about our country's natural treasures.

YCC members planting *hala* on Crater Hill.

USFWS biologist tends a high-tech Newell's Shearwater burrow, gathering valuable information about this threatened seabird's nesting habits.

Kauai's wildlife refuges provide excellent opportunities for environmental education.

## Kīlauea Point Natural History Association

Supporting the three refuges in the Kaua'i National Wildlife Refuge Complex is a "Friends" group known as Kīlauea Point Natural History Association (KPNHA). The Association is governed by a seven-member Board of Directors, and has a Memorandum of Agreement with the United States Fish and Wildlife Service (USFWS).

KPNHA is a 501(c)3 nonprofit whose mission is:

*To promote better understanding, appreciation, and conservation of the natural history and environment of Kauai's National Wildlife Refuges and native Hawaiian ecosystems by fostering educational, interpretive, and scientific activities and projects for the benefit of the public and wildlife.*

KPNHA runs the bookstore at the Kīlauea Point Visitor Center. Its profits support a wide range of activities and purchases in support of our mission. For example, KPNHA has funded scholarships for college students majoring in some field of environmental studies each year; geological and seabird research projects; school field trip transportation costs; the annual educational Ocean Fair; environmental education projects for local schools; the Kīlauea Point Lighthouse restoration project; and many different needs of the USFWS for Kauai's refuges.

A Web site was developed for KPNHA with information about the refuge, and links to other pertinent sites. You can check it out at:

www.kilaueapoint.com

Kīlauea Point National Wildlife Refuge is one of the most visited and scenic wildlife refuges in the nation. Please make it a point to pay us a visit! For those who would like to get involved, inquire about the Kīlauea Point volunteer program.

Kīlauea Point Natural History Association
P.O. Box 1130, Kīlauea, Kaua'i, HI 96754

Office phone: 808-828-0383

Kaua'i National Wildlife Refuge Complex office: 808-828-1413